Saving
Natural Theology
from Thomas Aquinas

Saving Natural Theology
from Thomas Aquinas

Jeffrey D. Johnson

FREE GRACE PRESS

Saving Natural Theology from Thomas Aquinas
Copyright © 2021 by Jeffrey D. Johnson

All rights reserved. No part of this book may be used or reproduced in any manner whatsoever without written permission except in the case of brief quotations embodied in critical articles and reviews. Direct your requests to the publisher at the following address:

Published by

Free Grace Press
3900 Dave Ward Dr., Ste. 1900
Conway, AR 72034
(501) 214-9663
email: support@freegracepress.com
website: www.freegracepress.com

Printed in the United States of America

Scripture quotations are from the ESV® Bible (The Holy Bible, English Standard Version®), copyright © 2001 by Crossway, a publishing ministry of Good News Publishers. Used by permission. All rights reserved.

ISBN: 978-1-952599-46-0

For additional Reformed Baptist titles, please email us for a free list or see our website at the above address.

Dedicated to
Owen Strachan
A Fearless Fighter

Contents

Preface		ix
Introduction		1
1.	Natural Revelation Is Not Natural Science	5
2.	The Natural Theology of Thomas Aquinas	13
3.	The Problems with the Natural Theology of Thomas Aquinas	27
4.	Greek Philosophy Is Unsavable	43
5.	The Apostle Paul's Rejection of Greek Philosophy	57
6.	Theologians Who Rejected Aquinas's Natural Theology	65
Conclusion		77

Preface

I am not convinced that natural theology, as a theological discipline, can be saved. I don't even know if it's a good idea to try to rescue it. Natural theology is closely linked to classical apologetics, and classical apologetics, due to the influence of Thomas Aquinas, is so interwoven with Greek philosophy that such associations may never be broken.

I am convinced that classical apologetics, being rooted in Greek philosophy, proves the wrong God. I am confident that a natural theology mixed with Greek philosophy is an utter failure. Thus, I titled my previous book on this subject *The Failure of Natural Theology: A Critical Appraisal of the Philosophical Theology of Thomas Aquinas.*[1]

---
1 Conway, AR: Free Grace Press, 2021.

As a presuppositionalist, I am convinced that revelation *alone* gets us to the only true and living God. Revelation includes both the book of nature and the book of Scripture. With this said, I am convinced that the book of nature (i.e., natural revelation) effectually reveals God to the natural man (Psalm 19; Romans 1).

I am convinced that natural revelation is the foundation for common grace, logic, mathematics, science, law, and knowledge in general. It is the underpinning for the structure of the family and is the glue that holds society together. For more on this, see the sections on two-kingdom theology in my books *What Every Christian Needs to Know about Social Justice*, *The Kingdom of God*, and *The Church*.[2]

I am convinced that, as Paul said, "nature itself teaches" us certain universal truths, such as traditional marriage and the roles of husbands and wives (1 Cor 11:14). I am persuaded that natural law is the foundation for civil authority (Rom 13:1–7). And based on what nature teaches, such as law written on our hearts, God will judge the nations in righteousness. And on that great day, no one will be able to say, "I didn't know God," or "I didn't know how God expected me to live."

---

[2] Conway, AR: Free Grace Press, 2021; Conway, AR: Free Grace Press, 2014; New Albany, MS: Media Grataie, 2020.

Saving Natural Theology from Thomas Aquinas | xi

Consequently, because I believe there is a body of doctrine communicated in natural revelation, I am convinced there is a theology communicated in nature. And it would seem natural to call this body of doctrine *natural theology*.

Presuppositionalists like myself are not against the body of doctrine communicated in natural revelation. We are against pagan philosophers who have suppressed, twisted, and perverted what has been communicated in natural revelation. Greek philosophers did not confess the God of natural revelation. Far from it. They rejected what they knew in their hearts by attempting to formulate their own explanation of God. They denied God's independence from the universe and his personal presence within the universe.

The god they created through their own finite speculations was an abstract being that is not the personal caretaker and judge of the universe. Such a deistic god is not the God of natural revelation.

Such pagan speculations, which run contrary to natural revelation, should never have been introduced into a Christian understanding of natural theology.

I blame Thomas Aquinas for ruining natural theology—not that Thomas was the first to mix Greek philosophy with theology, but he has done the most damage in syncretizing the pantheistic notions flowing out of Athens with the ontologically distinct and self-contained God who personally revealed himself in Jerusalem.

If natural theology can be saved, it must be saved from Thomas Aquinas. Therefore, if we can identify and root out the tentacles of Greek philosophy, which have so deeply penetrated this discipline, then it may be worth saving.

Honestly, I am not as concerned about saving the phrase *natural theology* as I am defending the charge often leveled at us presuppositionalists—that we reject natural revelation and natural law and the common grace that flows out of God's divine communication in nature.

As a presuppositionalist, I am convinced that our knowledge of God is dependent on divine revelation. It is impossible to reject what we know to be true from natural revelation, as did Plato and Aristotle, and afterward successfully work our way to a true understanding of God from the ground up. If we are going to know anything truly about God, we must begin with the knowledge that God has already revealed of himself to us.

I am convinced that the Bible affirms whatever the book of nature teaches us. Scripture goes beyond what natural revelation teaches, but natural revelation does not go beyond what Scripture teaches. If what we believe about God is not taught in Scripture, it must be rejected. As the Second London Baptist Confession of Faith states, "God alone is Lord of the conscience, and has left it free from the doctrines and commandments of men which are in anything contrary to his word, or not contained in it. So that to believe such doctrines, or obey such commands out of conscience, is to betray true liberty of conscience; and the requiring of an implicit faith, an absolute and blind obedience, is to destroy liberty of conscience and reason also" (21.2).

This is not biblicism—it's the biblical doctrine of the sufficiency of Scriptures.

Jeffrey D. Johnson
Pastor, Grace Bible Church,
President, Grace Bible Theological Seminary
Conway, AR

Introduction

What is natural theology? What is natural revelation? One thing is for certain: natural theology and natural revelation mean different things to different people. Some think natural theology is essentially the same as natural revelation. I have no problem with this. Others, such as Herman Bavinck, believe that natural theology can be logically constructed from natural revelation. I also have no problem with this.

But for Thomas Aquinas, long recognized as the person most closely associated with natural theology, natural theology has little to nothing to do with natural revelation—that is, at least in how the Bible defines natural revelation. As we shall see, instead of building his natural theology on natural revelation, Aquinas built his natural theology on natural science. And natural science (though good in what it does tell us) is not the same thing as natural revelation.

We need to do a few things to sort out the confusion. First, we must determine the attributes of natural revelation. Second, we need to contrast those attributes with the attributes of natural science. And third, after seeing that natural revelation and natural science are not the same, we must demonstrate why natural science (though good in explaining the physical universe) is not sufficient in telling us anything about the nature of the supernatural, spiritual, and transcendent God.

Principally, we will see that natural science, unlike natural revelation, cannot logically lead us to the *God of providence*. At best, when natural science is used to explain the nature of God, as with the various forms of Greek philosophy, it will lead to some form of deism or pantheism.

Again, if built on natural revelation as defined in Scripture, natural theology is sound, such as Herman Bavinck's. But a natural theology built on natural science, as laid out by Aquinas, is not sound. Such a foundation distorts the true knowledge of God. My goal in this book is not to critique the validity, efficacy, and usefulness of a natural theology rooted in natural revelation but to rescue natural theology from Thomas Aquinas. In other words, my objective is to make sure we construct our natural theology on natural revelation and not on natural science.

I

Natural Revelation Is Not Natural Science

This brings us to our first question: What is natural revelation? Or, more precisely, how does natural revelation work? Should we consider the scientific method, a multistep process of observing, hypothesizing, testing, and concluding, a part of divine revelation? Every scientific truth communicates something true about God. But is the empirical *method* of ascertaining scientific truth about sensible things the method God has chosen to universally reveal himself in nature? Thankfully, special revelation explains how natural revelation works. Principally, in Psalm 19, Romans 1, and Acts 17, we have objective knowledge of how God has chosen to reveal himself in nature. And from those passages, we learn a few things about natural revelation.

Natural Revelation Originates with God

First, God is the one who is communicating in natural revelation. The medium is not words but his created works. God's completed work—the sun, the stars, the mountains, the streams, the trees, the animals, and every other created thing—testifies of God's glory, power, and creativity. As the psalmist declares, "The heavens declare the glory of God, and the sky above proclaims his handiwork" (Ps 19:1).

Natural Revelation Is Universal

Second, we learn that natural revelation is universal. The psalmist continues by saying that "there is no speech, nor are there words, whose voice is not heard. Their voice goes out through all the earth, and their words to the end of the world" (Ps 19:3–4). As the heat of the sun touches everyone, natural revelation speaks to everyone.

Natural Revelation Is Efficacious

Third, we learn that God is good at getting his point across. God has revealed himself clearly, persuasively, and undeniably to everyone. No one can honestly say they did not understand the message of natural revelation. No one is ignorant, and no one is an honest agnostic or atheist. For this reason, Joel Beeke and Paul Smalley state, "General revelation is not a tool for Christians to convince people of something they do not know but to convict them of what they do know and fail to live up to."[1]

Natural Revelation Is Immediate

Fourth, we learn that there is no time lapse between God speaking and man understanding what God has spoken. All men have an immediate awareness of God. As Beeke and Smalley maintain, "general revelation is not potential revelation but actual revelation."[2] No discursive thinking, no syllogism, no inductive or deductive reasoning, no instruction, no argumentation, and no rational proof are needed for man to have an immediate awareness of God in nature. According to Herman Bavinck, man's knowledge of God "arises spontaneously and without coercion, without scientific argumentation and proof." Creation provides this knowledge to the educated and the uneducated alike. The old, young, and everyone in between are fully aware of God. Bavinck goes on to say, "Knowledge of God never needs to be instilled in people by coercion or violence, nor

---

1 Joel R. Beeke and Paul M. Smalley, *Reformed Systematic Theology: Revelation and God* (Wheaton: Crossway, 2019), 1:210.

2 Beeke and Smalley, 1:204.

by logical argumentation or compelling proofs, but belongs to humans by their very nature and arises spontaneously and automatically."[3] And according to Calvin, "there exists in the human mind and indeed by natural instinct, some sense of Deity [*sensus divinitatis*], we hold to be beyond dispute, since God himself, to prevent any man from pretending ignorance, has endued all men with some idea of his Godhead.... This is not a doctrine which is first learned at school, but one as to which every man is, from the womb, his own master; one which nature herself allows no individual to forget."[4]

Natural Revelation Is Continuous

Fifth, we learn that natural revelation is persistent. Like a constant ringing in the ear, God speaks in every moment of every day and every night. It is ceaseless communication. Creation is a relentless and unending testimony of God. "Day to day pours out speech, and night to night reveals knowledge" (Ps 19:2). Man cannot run or hide from the knowledge of God, which is continuously communicated everywhere and in everything. "Wherever you cast your eyes," John

---

3 Herman Bavinck, *Reformed Dogmatics*, trans. John Bolt and John Vriend (Grand Rapids: Baker Academic, 2003), 2:71, 73.

4 John Calvin, *Institutes of the Christian Religion*, ed. John T. McNeill, trans. Ford Lewis Battles (Philadelphia: Westminster, 1977). 1.3.1.

Calvin claimed, "there is no spot in the universe wherein you cannot discern at least some sparks of his glory." We may suppress the knowledge of God, but we cannot eliminate the divine communication found everywhere and in everything. As Calvin further remarked, "The whole world is a theater for the display of the divine goodness, wisdom, justice, and power" of God. Therefore, "we cannot open our eyes without being compelled to behold him."[5]

Natural Revelation Is Infallible

Sixth, we learn that natural revelation, as with all divine revelation, is infallible. Because revelation comes from the God who cannot err or lie, revelation, in all its forms, cannot be mixed with error or falsehoods. Though natural revelation does not tell us everything about God, what it does tell us about God is infallibly true.

In short, natural revelation extends and is limited to the infallible knowledge of God, which is revealed universally, effectually, immediately, and consistently.

Natural Science

On the other hand, natural science is not the same thing as natural revelation. First, the scien-

---

[5] Calvin, 1.5.1.

tific method can only explain physical realities. Although natural science is good in explaining the physical and materialistic universe, it cannot tell us anything sure about the nature of a supernatural and transcendent God. For instance, it can tell us much about the laws of nature and how motion works within material objects. But it cannot, through the use of the empirical senses, tell us anything about how God works. And the laws of science, though utilized by God as secondary causes in providence, cannot verify and affirm the existence of divine providence. In other words, science can tell us how physical things move and work, but it cannot tell us how God moves (or doesn't move) and work.

Second, unlike natural revelation, the scientific method is a fallible and multistep process of (1) empirical observation, (2) that leads to creating a hypothesis, (3) which then must be tested, (4) to come to a conclusion. Granted, there are many non-material realities that science has no way of verifying or rejecting, such as the laws of logic, mathematics, and ethics. Though science depends on these immaterial laws, science cannot prove them through its empirical method of ascertaining truth. So, it can be argued that science demands the existence of God to make sense of the laws of science, but it cannot rightly say anything about the nature of this God. Consequently, unlike natural revelation, what natural science empirically verifies as real and factual is not communicated universally, efficaciously, spontaneously, consistently, and infallibly from above.

Conclusion

In short, natural science and natural revelation are not the same things. The fundamental difference is this: science is a human achievement, while natural revelation is a gift from God.

2

THE NATURAL THEOLOGY OF THOMAS AQUINAS

Science and natural revelation are both good, but they are different. It is essential to note this because Aquinas constructed his natural theology on natural science rather than natural revelation. His version of natural theology was built not on the awareness of God spontaneously, efficaciously, universally, and infallibly revealed to all people in nature but on what he called a "philosophical science built up by human reason."[1] And according to Aquinas, this "philosophical science built up by

---

1 Thomas Aquinas, *Summa Theologica*, trans. Fathers of the English Dominican Province, rev. by Daniel J. Sullivan in "Great Books of the Western World," ed., Robert Maynard Hutchins (New York: Encyclopedia Britannica, 1952), 1.1.1.

human reason" is rooted in natural science—the study of how motion works in "sensible" things.

The Natural Theology of Aquinas Is Rooted in Natural Science

In contrast, Calvin taught that all knowledge begins with the awareness of God. "There is no knowing," Calvin famously claimed, "that does not begin with knowing God." The foundation of the knowledge of God is the starting point on which all other knowledge is established. Even science depends on God.

Yet Aquinas rejected the notion that all knowledge is founded on the knowledge of God. "The existence of God," Aquinas argued, "is not self-evident to us . . . [but] can be demonstrated from those of his effects which are known to us."[2] Etienne Gilson, one of the most renowned Thomist scholars, explained it this way: "Whether we start from the idea of God conceived in the human mind with St. Anselm, or from man and the world with St. Thomas, never, at any rate, do we start from God himself—He is invariably the goal."[3] Martin Grabmann, another important interpreter of Thomas, claimed, "The existence of God is . . . not an immediately self-evident, nor an

---

2 Aquinas, 1.2.2.
3 Etienne Gilson, *The Spirit of Mediaeval Philosophy* (Notre Dame, IN: University of Notre Dame, 1991), 85.

innate truth, but is a truth attained only by means of conclusion from premises."[4] For Aquinas, the starting point of our inquiring begins with what can be induced from sense experience. "According to the Philosopher [Aristotle]," argued Aquinas, "all our knowledge begins from the senses. Now [seeing that] God is furthest removed from the senses, . . . we do not know him first, but last."[5]

Therefore, according to Aquinas, for man to know God, he must start with the study of sensible things: "Now because we do not know the essence of God, the proposition is not self-evident to us; but needs to be demonstrated by things that are more known to us, though less known in their nature—namely, by effects." And this knowledge of the creative effects of God begins with our empirical senses: "Now it is natural to man to attain to intellectual truths through sensible objects," Aquinas claimed, "because all our knowledge originates from sense."[6] Thus, the nature of God—that which transcends the physical world—is derived from the study of the physical world.

---

[4] Martin Grabmann, *Thomas Aquinas: His Personality and Thought*, trans. Virgil Michel (New York: Longmans, Green, 1928), 99.

[5] *St Thomas Aquinas: Faith, Reason and Theology: Questions I-IV of His Commentary on the De Trinitate of Boethius*, trans. Armand Maurer (Toronto: Institute of Mediaeval Studies, 1987), 1.2.

[6] Aquinas, *Summa Theologica*, 1.2.1, 1.1.9.

Like Aristotle before him, Thomas placed his metaphysics *after* the study of the physical world and therefore called his natural theology a physical science built up by human reason. In other words, it is the knowledge of God that can be "scientifically known and demonstrated."[7]

And because Aquinas rooted natural knowledge of God not in divine revelation but in science, he admitted that such knowledge is not universally, efficaciously, spontaneously, persistently, and infallibly understood:

> If a truth of this nature were left to the sole enquiry of reason, three disadvantages would follow. One is that the knowledge of God would be confined to few. The discovery of truth is the fruit of studious enquiry. From this very many are hindered. Some are hindered by a constitutional unfitness, their natures being ill-disposed to the acquisition of knowledge.... These could not possibly spend time enough in the learned lessons of speculative enquiry to arrive at the highest point of human enquiry, the knowledge of God.... Thus, only with great labour of study is it possible to arrive at the searching out of the aforesaid truth; and this labour few are willing to undergo for sheer love of knowledge. Another disadvantage is that such as did arrive at the knowledge or discovery

---

7 Aquinas, 1.2.3, ad 1.

of the aforesaid truth would take a long time over it, on account of the profundity of such truth, and the many prerequisites to the study, and also because in youth and early manhood, the soul, tossed to and fro on the waves of passion, is not fit for the study of such high truth: only in settled age does the soul become prudent and scientific, as the Philosopher says. Thus, if the only way open to the knowledge of God were the way of reason, the human race would dwell long in thick darkness of ignorance: as the knowledge of God, the best instrument for making men perfect and good, would accrue only to a few, and to those few after a considerable lapse of time. A third disadvantage is that, owing to the infirmity of our judgement and the perturbing force of imagination, there is some admixture of error in most of the investigations of human reason. This would be a reason to many for continuing to doubt even of the most accurate demonstrations, not perceiving the force of the demonstration, and seeing the divers judgements of divers persons who have the name of being wise men.[8]

It is evident, therefore, that natural science and natural revelation are not to be confused.

---

[8] Thomas Aquinas, *Summa Contra Gentiles, Book I–II*, in Latin/English Edition of *The Works of Thomas Aquinas*, Vol. 11, trans. Fr. Laurence Shapcote (Green Bay: Aquinas Institute, 2018), 1.1.4. Also see Moses Maimonides, *Guide of the Perplexed*, trans. Shlomo Pines (Chicago: University of Chicago Press, 1966), 1.33.

The Natural Theology of Aquinas Is Built Up in Greek Philosophy

But how did Aquinas jump from physics to metaphysics, from science to philosophy? Borrowing from Aristotle, Aquinas argued that we can logically and philosophically reason our way from the nature of sensible things to the nature of the unsensible God. After empirically understanding how motion works in the universe, we can learn something true about God. But this means we must begin by empirically studying motion within the sensible things. For Aristotle, the study of the physical universe is the study of motion. "Nature has been defined," Aristotle claimed, "as a 'principle of motion and change.'"[9]

And what do we learn about sensible things in motion? According to Aristotle, we learn at least three things:

1. Sensible things in motion are contingent.

"Everything that is in motion must be moved by something. For if it has not the source of its motion in itself, it is evident that it is moved by something other than itself."[10]

---

9 Aristotle, *Physics*, in "Great Books of the Western World," gen. ed., Robert Maynard Hutchins, trans. R. P. Hardie and R. K. Gaye (New York: Encyclopedia Britannica, 1952), 3.1.

10 Aristotle, *Physics*, 7.1.

2. Sensible things in motion are mutable.

"Every motion is a change from one thing into something else."[11]

3. Sensible things in motion are not simple.

"Change is not found in all things but only between contraries and intermediates and contradictories."[12]

Based on this foundation, Aristotle attempted to reason up to the nature of God. Through his study of physics, Aristotle assumed that God was the opposite of all the attributes associated with physical things in motion. Because physics indicates that everything in motion must have an external cause, and because of the impossibility of an endless chain of external causes, God must be the motionless first cause of the universe. Since every sensible thing is moving and contingent, it must mean that movement makes things contingent. With immobility, epistemologically speaking, being the foundational attribute of Aristotle's understanding of God, Aquinas concluded along with Aristotle that God must not have any of the other attributes of motion—contingency, mutability, or complexity.

---

[11] Aristotle, *The Metaphysics: Books X-XIV*, in Loeb Classical Library, vol. 287, trans. Hugh Tredennick (Cambridge, MA: Harvard University Press, 1997), 11.12.4.

[12] Aristotle, *Metaphysics*, 11.11.3.

The Unmoved Mover Is Not the God of Natural Revelation.

Without any scientific exploration or logical syllogism, natural revelation immediately and universally discloses that God is the personal creator (Romans 1) and governor of the universe (Acts 17). But for Aristotle, the "unmoved mover" is logically neither of these two things.

The Unmoved Mover Is Not the Personal Creator of the Universe.

According to the logic of Aristotle, the unmoved mover is not the personal creator of the universe. How did the immobile God set the universe in motion if he couldn't move? The answer, at least according to Aristotle, is that God did not set the universe in motion. Putting something in motion would require motion in God, and such motion would prevent him from being the *unmoved* mover. As Aristotle claimed, "the instrument of motion [the efficient cause] must both move something else and be itself in motion."[13]

Thus, for Aristotle, God cannot be the universe's instrumental cause (efficient/moving cause) because God would cease to be immobile if he exerted any free acts of power. If God exerted

---

13   Aristotle, *Physics*, 8.5.

any power or force or energy, even in the slighted degree, he would cease to be the unmoved mover.

For Aristotle, God is not the efficient cause of the universe because he cannot exert any unnecessary power or energy. Rather, he is what Aristotle called the final cause of the cosmos. Aristotle imagined that the final cause is the ultimate good to which all things aspire and desire. Why is the universe in motion? What is the motivation behind all the endless energy moving things from one state of being to other states of being? It is the final cause—God—a perfect being without change or actualization.

Aristotle believed that, in all things desiring their own actuality, they are desiring God (even if they are unaware of it). This brings us to how the unmoved mover can move things without moving himself. Like the pull of a magnet, the unmoved mover remains completely passive and unaware that he is exciting objects to move after him. Simply put, God incites movement by being the ultimate object of desire.

Aristotle explained it this way: "The first principle and primary reality [God] is immovable, both essentially and accidentally, but it excites the primary form of motion, which is one and eternal. Now since that which is moved must be moved by something, and the prime mover must be essentially immovable, and eternal motion must be excited by something eternal, and one motion by some one thing."[14]

Aristotle further stated that God "causes motion as being an object of love." This means that things in motion cannot help but love God, but God cannot love things in motion. Nevertheless, in this way, God moves things without moving at all: "Now it [God] moves in the following manner. The object of desire and the object of thought move without being moved."[15]

Thus, reasoning from natural science to God led Aristotle to conclude that the unmoved mover was not the creator of the universe. For Aristotle, the universe (and all the motion within it) is eternal. But this also means that for Aristotle, God is not personal or relational. This deistic and unconcerned God is not the personal ruler and judge of the universe.

The god of Aristotle is impersonal because he is immobile. According to Aristotle, the unmoved mover can do nothing but remain in a single, timeless, and necessary act of self-contemplation. This is altogether different than the personal God of natural and special revelation.

---

14 Aristotle, *Metaphysics*, 12.8.3–4.
15 Aristotle, 12.7.4; 12.7.2.

The Unmoved Mover Is Not the Providential Governor of the Universe.

Hence, the god of Aristotle, according to B. A. G. Fuller, "knows only himself with a knowledge in which there is distinction neither of self from not-self, nor of the activity of thought as such from its content." "All God's life and thought," Fuller goes on to explain, "are locked up. He knows nothing but it, nothing but himself."[16] With such a god as this, Aristotle turns things backward. The cosmos somehow can aspire after God, but God knows nothing of the cosmos. Aristotle's god is oblivious and indifferent about the affairs of men.

For Aristotle, mobility equals contingency. Because movement is found in all contingent things, movement must be what makes things contingent. For Aristotle, mobility also equals mutability. Because movement is found in all mutable things, movement must be what makes things mutable. For Aristotle, movement also equals complexity. Because movement is found in all complex things, movement must be what makes things complex.

Thus, Aristotle did not believe the unmoved mover could be the moving cause of the universe,

---

16 B. A. G. Fuller, "The Theory of God in Book Λ of Aristotle's Metaphysics," in *The Philosophical Review*, Vol. 16, No. 2 (Mar 1907), 173, 175.

and he assumed any such movement (such as the free act of creating the universe) would make God mutable, complex, and contingent.

For Aristotle, God is not just simple and immutable in his essence, which is biblical. His simplicity and immutability also include his operations and activity and works, which is not biblical. In other words, for Aristotle, God's operations, activity, and works are identical to his simple essence. God is not just who he is; God is what he does. He is pure act. Thus, God cannot do anything other than what he is, which is the timeless act of self-existing in the simple static state of self-contemplation.

The Natural Theology of Aquinas Is Corrected by Revealed Theology

Following Aristotle, Aquinas laid the foundation of his natural theology in natural science and, from there, attempted to make the philosophical transition from physics to metaphysics. In so doing, Aquinas embraced the metaphysical notion that God is immobile. But realizing that the Bible teaches that God is the providential governor of the universe in which he created out of nothing, he used the Bible to guide and correct his natural theology from the unorthodoxy of Aristotle.

Aquinas admitted that reason alone, based on the study of sensible things in motion, does not logically lead to a personal creator who governs the universe. This was a matter of sacred doctrine only revealed in the Bible. "That there is one God can be proved by reason," according to Aquinas, "but that God has an immediate providence over all things . . . is a matter of faith."[17]

Conclusion

What is the natural theology of Aquinas? In short, it's not the body of teaching revealed in natural revelation. Rather, for Aquinas, natural theology is all that which can be rationally deduced from natural science, guided by pagan philosophy, and corrected by biblical orthodoxy.

---

[17] Thomas Aquinas, *Compendium Theologiae*. Trans. Cyril Vollert, S.J. Ed. Paul A. Böer, Sr. (Edmond, OK: Veritatis Splendor, 2012), 2.246.

3

The Problems with the Natural Theology of Thomas Aquinas

Because Aquinas constructed his natural theology on a different foundation than divine revelation, he introduced numerous problems into his theology proper. By seeking to baptize the metaphysics of Aristotle, Thomas actually ended up paganizing the God of revelation. But such paganization is the natural result of the problems of Aquinas's natural theology.

The Natural Theology of Aquinas Doesn't Lead to the God of Revelation

The natural theology of Aristotle and Aquinas

does not lead to the God of natural or special revelation. It only leads to a deistic and apathetic being who cannot create and govern the universe. Without the aid of "sacred doctrine," Aquinas's natural theology remains unorthodox. And if this is the case, it's a failed natural theology. For if one's natural theology does not arrive at the same God of natural and special revelation, it doesn't need to be corrected but instead rejected.

The Natural Theology of Aquinas Is Not Founded on Natural Revelation

According to Paul, natural revelation reveals that God is the God of providence (Acts 17:26). We don't need the Bible to know that God is the one overseeing history! Yet Aquinas admitted that what is clearly and immediately and universally revealed in nature could not be "scientifically known and demonstrated" from reason alone. According to Aquinas, divine providence is revealed only in special revelation. And this alone demonstrates that Aquinas did not build his natural theology on natural revelation but on the physics and metaphysics of Aristotle.

Herman Bavinck identified the main difference between the natural theology of Aquinas and the natural theology of the Reformers when he stated, "Whereas natural theology was originally an account, in light of Scripture, of what Christians can know concerning God from creation, it soon became an exposition of what nonbelieving rational persons could learn from nature by the power of their own reasoning. In other words, natural theology became rational theology." But, according to Bavinck, "there is no such thing as a separate natural theology that could be obtained apart from any revelation solely on the basis of a reflective consideration of the universe. The knowledge of God that is gathered up in so-called natural theology is not the product of human reason."[1]

In other words, the natural theology of the Reformers was built on natural revelation, while Aquinas built his natural theology on natural science and Greek philosophy. According to Bavinck,

> a distinct natural theology, obtained apart from any revelation, merely through observation and study of the universe in which man lives, does not exist.... Scripture urges us to behold heaven and earth, birds and ants, flowers and lilies, in order that we may see and recognize God in them. "Lift up your eyes on high, and see who hath created these" (Isa 40:26). Scripture does not reason in the abstract. It does not make God the conclusion of a syllogism, leaving it to us whether we

---

[1] Bavinck, *Reformed Dogmatics*, 2:78, 74.

> think the argument holds or not. But it speaks with authority. Both theologically and religiously it proceeds from God as the starting point.
>
> We receive the impression that belief in the existence of God is based entirely upon these proofs. But indeed that would be "a wretched faith, which, before it invokes God, must first prove his existence." The contrary, however, is the truth. There is not a single object the existence of which we hesitate to accept until definite proofs are furnished. Of the existence of self, of the world round about us, of logical and moral laws, etc., we are so deeply convinced because of the indelible impressions which all these things make upon our consciousness that we need no arguments or demonstration. Spontaneously, altogether involuntarily: without any constraint or coercion, we accept that existence of God. The so-called proofs are by no means the final grounds of our most certain conviction that God exists. This certainty is established only by faith; that is, by the spontaneous testimony which forces itself upon us from every side.[2]

The failure of natural science to tell us anything about the inward workings of God is not due to the Enlightenment but to the inherent inadequacy of the empirical senses.

---

2 Herman Bavinck, *The Doctrine of God* (Grand Rapids: Eerdmans, 1951), 78–79.

The Natural Theology of Aquinas Is Founded on a Leap of Logic

Moreover, if God is transcendent and ontologically distinct from the universe, then it's a huge leap to jump from earth to heaven. I am convinced it's an impossible leap. Yet, Aristotle transitioned from physics to metaphysics by making a philosophical assumption. Without having the faith to believe that God created the world out of nothing, Aristotle assumed that the cause-and-effect relationship between sensible things flowed back to the first cause. That is, he assumed that the laws of physics apply to God as much as they apply to sensible things.

Rather than an ontologically self-contained God that remains distinct from the universe, Aristotle based his philosophy on the pagan idea God and all things in the universe are connected and united through a chain of being. Consequently, he assumed that the laws of physics apply to God as much as they apply to sensible things. Aristotle assumed that power and movement work within contingent things in the same way they work in a non-contingent God.

Of course, the cosmological argument proves the necessity of a non-contingent being (i.e., God). But the cosmological argument does not prove, one way or another, if this non-contingent being is self-moving or unmoving. The cosmological argument has no way of knowing if there is motion in God or not. Yes, there is not an autonomous self-moving being within the physical universe. But just because there is no self-moving being in the universe does not rule out the possibility of a self-contained, autonomous (Trinitarian) Being who can independently move, act, create, govern, and destroy according to his own good pleasure.

Just maybe God doesn't need any external power to be able to freely exercise his own power. Just because all delegated and contingent powers depend on external power for their movement does not mean that the omnipotent and self-contained God must remain motionless to remain non-contingent.

Of course, science cannot tell us one way or the other if God is immobile or self-moving. And thus, Herman Bavinck placed his finger on the problem when he stated, "We have no right . . . to apply the law of causality to such a first cause, and that we therefore cannot say anything specific about it."[3]

This is not just Bavinck's opinion. This is the conclusion of some of the most notable Thomist and Dominican scholars throughout history. One of the leading Thomist scholars of our day, Ed-

---
3 Bavinck, *Reformed Dogmatics*, 2:82.

ward Feser, admitted, "I do deny that arguments grounded in natural science alone can get you to classical theism."[4] And according to Edward Gilson, "it does not follow from the fact that there is a first Mover, unmoved from outside, that there exists a first Mover who is absolutely immobile. Hence Aristotle points out that the expression 'a first Mover, not set in motion' is ambiguous. It can, in the first place, mean an absolutely immobile first Mover; in that case our conclusion holds. But it can also mean that this first Mover receives no movement from outside, while conceding that it may move itself."[5] Though the cosmological argument may get us to a non-contingent being, it cannot explain how this being is non-contingent.

The Natural Theology of Aquinas Added an Extra Attribute to God

Divine immobility is not something revealed in either natural or special revelation. But because Aquinas built his natural theology on natural science and Greek philosophy, he ended up adding an extra attribute—immobility—to the simple and immutable essence of God. But this had its troubling consequences.

---

[4] Edward Feser, *Essays, Neo-scholastic* (South Bend, IL: St Augustine's Press, 2015), 62.

[5] Edward Gilson, *The Philosophy of St. Thomas Aquinas*, ed. G. A. Elrington, trans. Edward Bullough (New York: Dorset, 1948), 75.

Divine Simplicity Engulfs All God's Diverse Operations and Activity

For Aquinas, divine simplicity is not restricted to God's essence (as the Bible teaches). It's true that God is all that he is "without body, parts, or passions."[6] Divine simplicity is a vital doctrine to uphold. I am personally convinced of this.

But Aquinas incorporated God's activity (i.e., the free exercise of his will and power) into the doctrine of simplicity. God supposedly "freely" willed the universe into existence in the same undifferentiated act of willing his eternal existence. "In willing himself primarily," Aquinas stated, "he wills all other things."[7] God's simple essence and complex activity of creating and governing the universe essentially becomes identical for Aquinas because God cannot have movement. He can only be and do what he is. Or to put it another way, God is what he does.

This is an extreme form of simplicity that logically leads to pantheism—a God that cannot *not* create or relate. God is not simply "I am who I am." For Aquinas, God is what he does—as if

---

[6] Second London Baptist Confession of Faith, 2.1.

[7] Thomas Aquinas, "Summa Contra Gentiles, Book I–II," in Latin/English Edition of the *Works of Thomas Aquinas*, Vol. 11, trans. Fr. Laurence Shapcote (Green Bay: Aquinas Institute, 2018), 1.75.

God revealed himself to Moses by declaring, "I am what I do."

Divine Immutability Engulfs All God's Diverse Operations and Activity

In addition to that unbiblical concept, divine immutability, according to Aquinas, is also not restricted to God's essence. Like divine simplicity, immutability is a critical doctrine to affirm and uphold. God's nature cannot change (Mal 3:6). I am personally convinced of this as well.

Aquinas, however, did not restrict immutability to the essence of God but extended it to God's operations, activity, and works. Again, this is because God cannot move. Thus, for Aquinas, divine immutability is synonymous with divine immobility. But Aquinas couldn't reconcile this with the doctrine of creation because any free act of the volition in God, such as creating the world out of nothing, would necessitate movement in God's will. And such a movement in God's will would necessitate a change in God's essence.

But nowhere in natural or special revelation is movement, in and of itself, depicted as an imperfection. Rather than depicting God in a constant state of motionlessness, the Bible describes the self-contained, ontological Godhead as alive. Each of the three persons are actively and eternally loving and glorifying one another. The Puritan William Perkins identified the life of God as that "by which the Divine nature is in perpetual action, living, and *moving in itself.*"[8]

Therefore, according to Herman Bavinck, immutability "should not be confused with monotonous sameness or rigid immobility."[9] Charles Hodge says, "Theologians, in their attempts to state, in philosophical language, the doctrine of the Bible on the unchangeableness of God, are apt to confound immutability with immobility. In denying that God can change, they seem to deny that He can act."

"We know," Hodge goes on to explain, "that God is immutable in his being, his perfections, and his purposes; and we know that He is perpetually active. And, therefore, activity and immutability must be compatible; and no explanation of the latter inconsistent with the former ought to be admitted."[10]

More recently, Louis Berkhof stated, "The divine immutability should not be understood as

---

8 William Perkins, "A Golden Chain," in *The Works of William Perkins,* ed. Joel Beeke (Grand Rapids: Reformation Heritage Books, 2019), 6:15. Italics mine.

9 Bavinck, *Reformed Dogmatics,* 2:158.

10 Charles Hodge, *Systematic Theology* (Grand Rapids: Eerdmans, 1981), 1:391.

implying *immobility*, as if there was no movement in God."[11]

We must affirm the immutability and simplicity of God's essence, but we mustn't collapse God's essence with God's operations and activity. Otherwise, God is no longer the personal creator and governor of the universe. Therefore, we should not build our understanding of divine simplicity and immutability from the philosophical notion of a *hierarchical chain of being*. Like Aristotle, this would lead to divine immobility and pantheism.

Instead, we should root our understanding of divine simplicity and immutability from within the knowledge of an ontologically distinct God who freely created the universe out of nothing. This is because simplicity and immutability don't mean the same thing in a pantheistic worldview as they do in a biblical worldview that is built on an ontological, distinct, and self-contained God who personally oversees the affairs of the world.

Aquinas verbally maintained the doctrine of creation and divine providence. But because he rooted his knowledge of God in Aristotelian philosophy, his theology was filled with irresolvable tension and contradictions. I address these critical illogicalities in my book *The Failure of Natural*

---

[11] Louis Berkhof, *Systematic Theology* (Grand Rapids: Eerdmans, 1996), 59.

Theology: A Critical Appraisal of the Philosophical Theology of Thomas Aquinas.

For our purposes in this book, however, we can reduce the tension in Aquinas's theology to his doctrine of divine immobility. It was logically impossible for Aquinas to maintain God's immobility with God's operations and activity without having to constant resist the gravitational pull of pantheism. So much so, he wrote a book toward the end of his life called *Disputed Questions on the Power of God* in which he cataloged the various difficulties—chiefly the difficulty of a temporal and unnecessary universe created out of nothing.

Aquinas admitted that *creatio ex nihilo* cannot be demonstrated by reason alone. If we are going to build all our knowledge on science rather than on the God of natural and special revelation, an eternal universe would be the logical conclusion. This, then, is the logical conclusion of Aristotle's philosophy; for something, he supposed, cannot come from nothing. And when logically trying to resolve this with the biblical account of creation, Aquinas conveniently responded by saying the rules of motion (in this case) do not apply to God:

> The Philosopher says that it is a common axiom or opinion of the physicists that from nothing nothing is made, because the natural agent, which was the object

of their research, does not act except by movement. Consequently there must needs be a subject of movement or change which, as we have stated, is not required for a supernatural agent.[12]

In so doing, Aquinas asserted that the rules that apply to finite things in motion do not apply to the unmoved mover (see QDP, 2 and 3), which is true. But Aquinas was not consistent in applying this principle. If God transcends the laws of motion that govern the physical world, why did he base his understanding of God on these laws in the first place? Why not apply this principle at the beginning of his natural theology by rejecting his epistemological foundation of empiricism? It sure would have made his job much easier for him.

Aquinas believed we could learn that God is the unmoved mover by studying the principles of motion within sensible things, but when these same principles make it impossible for the unmoved mover to be the creator of an unnecessary and temporal universe, they are no longer useful in telling us anything more about how the supernatural God operates.

Josef Pieper, another important Dominican Thomist, recognized the considerable amount

---

12 Thomas Aquinas, *Quaestiones Disputatae De Potentia Dei*, trans. English Dominican Fathers (Westminster, MD: The Newman Press, 1952), 2. Reply to 1.

of tension in Aquinas's doctrine of God when he concluded, "His endeavor was fraught with a multitude of potential conflicts; that it would be a source of virtually incalculable difficulties and discords which could scarcely ever be brought to a final 'harmony.'"[13]

The Natural Theology of Aquinas Is Dependent on Greek Philosophy

The natural theology of Aquinas is not just rooted in natural science; it is dependent on pagan philosophy. And we have seen that the god of Aquinas's favorite philosopher was not a god anywhere close to resembling the God of natural and special revelation.

Conclusion

All these problems are the result of *not* building his natural theology on the foundation of the knowledge of God that God himself revealed in nature. Aquinas looked to a pagan philosopher rather than looking to God. In so doing, Aquinas introduced deistic and pantheistic concepts into the Christian worldview in which they do not belong.

We must remember that the beginning of wisdom, as Solomon said, is the fear of God (Prov

---

13 Pieper, *Guide to Thomas Aquinas*, 118.

9:10). Consequently, if we love wisdom (i.e., philosophy), let us start by bowing our knee in fear to the clear and universal knowledge that God has already revealed to us. If we don't build our epistemology on this foundation, then we should not expect to arrive at a proper understanding of God.

4

GREEK PHILOSOPHY IS UNSAVABLE

If we mean by the term *natural theology* that which is built on natural revelation, then natural theology is worth saving. If, however, we mean that which was done by pagan philosophers and synthesized with revealed theology, then such a natural theology is not worth saving. A natural theology integrated with Greek philosophy is not worth saving because Greek philosophy is unsavable. This is because, in all of its various forms, Greek philosophy wasn't constructed on natural revelation.

What God revealed of himself in nature, the Greek philosophers rejected. What they knew without proof or demonstration, they disallowed to try to construct their own false god with demonstration and logical proofs.

But demonstration and logical proofs are only as good as their starting premise. It doesn't matter how tightly argued a logical proof may be. If the starting presupposition is faulty, the whole argument is faulty.

And apparently, the pagan philosophers didn't want to begin with the knowledge of God that had already been given to them. Rather, they wanted to build their conception of god from scratch—from the ground up.

One may object and claim that the pagan philosophers only wanted to prove what they already knew in their hearts. But, as we shall see, the god they sought to prove was not anywhere close to resembling the God they knew in their hearts.

The True God of Natural Revelation

Thankfully, God didn't leave it to man to construct his theology from scratch. Though natural revelation does not tell us everything we need to know about God, such as that he is Trinitarian, it does provide us with a basic knowledge of his existence, his nature, and his relationship to the universe and ourselves.

God's Existence

God has made it clear that he exists (Ps 19:1). No one, Paul says, is without excuse (Rom 1:20). As John Blanchard has famously said, "God doesn't believe in atheists."

God's Nature

But not only do we know that God exists, we know he is transcendent and absolute (Acts 17:25), infinite (Acts 17:24), and all-powerful (Rom 1:20). In other words, all humanity knows that God is self-contained and ontologically distinct from the universe. Though they may not have confessed it, the Greek philosophers knew this as well.

God's Relationship to the Universe

Mankind also knows that this ontologically distinct and self-contained God is not an unknowable deistic force. Natural revelation tells us that God is the personal Creator. All men know that God, in great wisdom and power and glory, created the universe (Ps 19:1; Rom 1:20). The God of natural revelation is not only a transcendent God but the God of natural revelation is also an imminent God who is near and cares (Acts 17:27). In other words, the God of natural revelation is not like the god of Plato and Aristotle, a god who is distinct and unconcerned about the affairs of this world. The God of revelation is a God who is sovereign over all the affairs that take place within the universe (Acts 17:26). God is ever present, for all men know that God is their provider and is watching all that they do.

This God, as we have already noted multiple times, is the God of divine providence. For, as Paul said, "he did not leave himself without witness, for he did good by giving you rains from heaven and fruitful seasons, satisfying your hearts with food and gladness" (Acts 14:17). This too was something the Greek philosophers knew in their hearts but suppressed in their writings in unrighteousness.

God's Relationship to Humanity

Because the God of revelation is deeply concerned about the affairs of the universe, all mankind knows they're in trouble with God. They all know God is righteous (Ps 97:6; Rom 1:18) and angry with those, like themselves, who have sinned against him (Rom 1:18).

They know they are sinners because natural revelation continuously reveals God's universal law in their consciences (Rom 2:15). Thus, men know that they have fallen short of God's standard and are guilty and without excuse before a holy, just, and angry God who will hold them personally accountable (Rom 2:15).

In essence, natural revelation reveals everything we need to know to be without excuse. It reveals God's glory and our guilt. It reveals our hopelessness. Natural revelation cannot save us, but it reveals our need for salvation.

The Doctrinal Baseline

If natural theology is built on natural revelation, then the knowledge communicated in natural revelation is the doctrinal baseline. Whatever else can be logically deduced from the knowledge of a personal God, the knowledge of a personal God is the minimum of what natural theologians must confess if they are going to build their natural theology on natural revelation. In other words, if any philosopher does not confess an ontologically distinct God who is personally involved in overseeing the affairs of the world, we can be certain that philosopher didn't build their natural theology on natural revelation.

The Pagan Gods of Greek Philosophy

If we build a theology below the doctrinal baseline freely revealed to us in the book of nature, then we are not building a theology on natural revelation. Instead, we are rejecting what we already know to be true and suppressing the truth in unrighteousness. And we shouldn't expect to find the light when we are knowingly running into the darkness. That is, those who reject the knowledge of a personal and ontologically distinct God at the beginning of their natural theology will never arrive at a personal and ontologically distinct God at the conclusion of their natural theology.

This is because, as I explain in *The Failure of Natural Theology*, without the knowledge that God is Trinitarian, it is impossible for even the smartest men on earth to be able to reconcile how God is both ontologically transcendent and personally immanent in his providential care over the affairs of men.[1]

But we don't need the Bible and its Trinitarian solution to know that God is both absolute and personally relatable. It is sufficient that God has revealed himself in nature, without rational explanation, that he is both. Man does not have to be able to reconcile these two truths to know in his heart they are both indeed true.

But the Greek philosophers were not content to leave their knowledge of God to that which is communicated to them by God. They were not content to trust God. They, in their finite minds, wanted to explain the existence of all things. They in their pride wanted to explain the ultimate meaning of all things, even if this meant they had

---

1 See Johnson, *The Failure of Natural Theology*, chap. 1.

to undermine and suppress the knowledge of God communicated to them in natural revelation.

Their suppression of natural revelation is fairly easy to prove by a brief overview of the history of Greek philosophy. What we discover is not a few errors easily corrected but various pantheistic or deistic worldviews inherently incoherent at the foundational level.

The Pre-Socratics

It doesn't take long to notice that none of the pre-Socratic philosophers confessed to believing in the God of natural revelation. What was revealed to them in nature was rejected by them in their explanation of nature. They, in their reasoning and philosophical speculations, did not acknowledge an ontologically distinct and personal God who is providentially in control over the affairs of the universe. Instead, they viewed the creation rather than the Creator as the primary principle and the final explanation and the ultimate cause of everything. For Thales, it was water; for Anaximander, air; for Heraclitus, fire; and for Empedocles, the ultimate cause of everything was earth.

Of course, this is a far cry for anything resembling the God of Psalm 19 and Romans 1 and 2. Though they may have spoken of this ultimate principle with divine-like properties, it is impossible to ontologically separate their primary principle (i.e., god) from the universe itself. Thus, the pre-Socratics advocated a form of impersonal pantheism, not the personal God of natural revelation.

Socrates, Plato, and Aristotle

Socrates, Plato, and Aristotle built philosophies a bit more complex, but they too did not come close to confessing the God of natural revelation.

For Plato, the most godlike being is a figure he called Demiurge, who crafted the universe out of the eternal and shapeless material after the patterns of the eternal and abstract "Forms." But Demiurge is not like the God of the Bible. One, Demiurge is subordinate to the abstract Forms. And the abstract Forms exist in a hierarchy, with the highest being the Form of the Good. Second, like the Forms, the material universe is also eternal. The god of Plato, if he can even be called a god, is dependent on the eternal Forms, which are above him, and dependent on the eternal matter, which is below him. Thus, the god of Plato is not the absolute and independent, ontological, self-contained, personal God of natural revelation.

Aristotle's god, as we have already seen, is not any more personal and relatable than the god of Plato. He is neither the creator nor the governor of the universe. Most importantly, the god of Aristotle is not the righteous judge of mankind.

The foundational error of Greek philosophy is its failure to acknowledge that God and the universe are not ontologically distinct. In other words, in Greek philosophy, there is no Creator/creature distinction. In all their rationalizations, explanations, and speculations, the ultimate being remains ontologically linked to the universe through some type of chain of being. And, in so doing, their understanding of the ultimate being is impersonally unconcerned with the affairs of humanity.

In a word, Greek philosophy, in all its forms, denies the doctrine of divine providence revealed in natural revelation. But most importantly, the Greek philosophers did away with any real meaning of sin, judgment, and divine punishment in their intellectual pursuits. The basic message of natural revelation—that man is hopelessly guilty and will be held accountable to the personal and righteous and holy God, who is the creator and governor of the universe—they rejected. These philosophers didn't assist their students in seeing their need for salvation.

This makes Greek philosophy not a handmaiden but a hindrance to special theology. In other words, pagan philosophers rejected the light of nature and assisted the kingdom of darkness in advancing false doctrines.

Is Greek Philosophy Salvageable?

Regardless of these blatant errors, Thomas Aquinas remained convinced that Greek philosophy had touched on enough truth for it to remain useful for theology. And the errors, as we have seen for Aquinas, can be corrected by Christian orthodoxy.

Yet, as we have also seen, Aquinas confused a natural theology built on natural revelation with a natural theology built on natural science, not to mention his failure to rid his theology of the pantheistic error of divine immobility.

Similarly, in his attempt to redeem Greek philosophy, David Haines confuses a natural theology built on natural revelation with a natural theology built on Greek philosophy in his book *Natural Theology: A Biblical and Historical Introduction and Defense*. For instance, after Haines provides a solid explanation of natural revelation, he goes on to argue for the validity and usefulness of Greek philosophy:

> If this interpretation of Scripture's teaching on natural theology is correct, then we should be able to examine the history of pagan thought and see philosophers and

> theologians discovering something about God through observations of nature. We need not expect perfect or complete knowledge, merely some sort of partial and incomplete knowledge of truths about the existence and nature of the divine.[2]

Haines admits, after surveying the history of Greek philosophy, that pagan philosophers conflated their understanding of the ultimate being with the universe itself. But, for Haines, their pantheistic conclusions were not sufficient reason to outright reject Greek philosophy. "Many theologians," Haines writes, "have noted that Greek philosophical discussions about God are riddled not only with errors, but with incoherencies. This is most certainly true." But, according to Haines, "this imperfect knowledge of God is exactly what we would expect," and incomplete and imperfect knowledge of God, mixed with some false claims, is not enough deem Greek philosophy as unredeemable. In a way of explanation, Haines said that because "someone has made some false claims about something does not imply that every statement that has been made by that person about the thing in question is false. Rather, it is very possible (in fact, it happens all the time) to know some truths about something or someone,

---

[2] David Haines, *Natural Theology: A Biblical and Historical Introduction and Defense* (Landrum, SC: Davenant, 2021), 44-45.

and, at the same time, to believe false statements about that thing or person to be true."[3]

And I would agree with Haines if we were merely talking about secondary errors and a few false claims about tertiary matters. But we are looking at fatal errors on the foundational level. For instance, if an eyewitness to an automobile accident can't rightly recall the precise shade of color of the car that ran the stoplight, this does not mean the person is an untrustworthy witness. But if the eyewitness is wrong about what city the car accident took place, then nothing else he says can be trusted.

Likewise, when it comes to Greek philosophers, we are not talking about the degree of personal control God has over pain, suffering, and evil. Such errors could be easily corrected without dismissing their entire philosophical system. Instead, we are talking about whether God is personal or an abstract impersonal force. This is not a slight disagreement but a foundation pillar of an antithetical worldview.

Conclusion

In short, Greek philosophy is unsavable because its errors are not restricted to a few minor and secondary differences with the God of revelation.

---

[3] Haines, 178.

It is, however, in all its various forms, an intellectual attack upon the God of revelation. Thus, Greek philosophy is not something that can be repaired and redeemed by the Christian theologian. It is an intellectual system of darkness that must be rejected altogether. Pagan philosophy, in all its diverse forms, is antithetical to the God of natural and special revelation.

Consequently, Christian theologians, such as Aquinas, who build their natural theology on Greek philosophy end up synthesizing pantheistic concepts and ideas into their theology proper. And this type of natural theology must not be saved but rejected.

5

THE APOSTLE PAUL'S REJECTION OF GREEK PHILOSOPHY

What more do we need than the words of Scripture that warn against looking to the philosophy of the so-called wise men of this world? As the apostle Paul wrote in his epistle to the Colossians, "see to it that no one takes you captive by philosophy and empty deceit, according to human tradition, according to the elemental spirits of the world, and not according to Christ" (Col 2:8). And to the Corinthians, "Where is the one who is wise? Where is the scribe? Where is the [philosopher] of this age? Has not God made foolish the wisdom of the world?" (1 Cor 1:20).

Those who think the apostle Paul appealed to Greek philosophy in his Mars Hill address fail to realize that Paul dismantled the foundational presupposition of Greek philosophy in this address. Though Paul was addressing a mixed group of thinkers who enjoyed discussing new ideas and arguing among themselves about their differences, they all held at least one idea in common. They all believed the ultimate being—the being behind all other beings—is impersonal, deistic, and unknowable. In other words, though the Epicureans and Stoics debated on how best to live in a materialistic universe, they both agreed that knowledge is restricted to the empirical and materialistic universe. Thus, God remains utterly hidden and out of reach.

Their agreement in this matter was rooted in the fact that both Epicureanism and Stoicism can be traced back to the metaphysics of Aristotle. Because of this common ground, Epicureans and Stoics agreed the universe was not created by a personal, knowable, and ontologically distinct God.

Likewise, the polytheists (those who worshiped idols) who were present at Mars Hill also agreed with the Epicureans and Stoics in the unknowability of the ultimate being. In agreement with Aristotle, they did not believe in a personal and ontologically distinct and self-contained God who created the world out of nothing. And, as with Aristotle and Plato, they assumed there was a chain of being that ontologically linked the ultimate being with all other beings.

Therefore, though the ultimate being is ineffable, it is possible to know something about God by knowing something about those things that share and participate in his "being." Every materialistic thing in the universe (the sun, the moon, and even people) shares and participates in the being of God. Or, conversely, the unknowable God participates in every knowable thing. Consequently, though it is impossible to directly connect and relate to and know the impersonal God, it is possible to interact with, relate to, and know the materialistic things that ontologically flow from and out of God.

Thus, polytheists, based on the notion that God is in all things, concluded that all things are worthy of worship. And, as their thinking goes, by worshiping the sun, the moon, and other such things, they were indirectly worshiping the unknown and out of reach God. Because God is not ontologically distinct from every diverse material thing, graven images made from material things such as wood, silver, and good are also proper to worship. In fact, graven images are more accessible to worshipers.

In his discourse at Mars Hill, therefore, Paul was not trying to find "common ground" between the Christian God and the unknowable God of pagan philosophy. Rather, Paul started his address by placing his finger on the one notion that all his hearers and pagan worshipers held in common—that the ultimate being is unknowable. Then immediately afterward, Paul claimed they were all wrong. They, according to Paul, were not just wrong in the things they disagreed with among themselves (such as how to live and worship) but also, and more importantly, in the one thing they held in common—the very foundation of their worldview.

Greek philosophy is wrong, Paul is essentially saying, at the foundational level. God is not unknowable for God has revealed himself in nature and in Christ. Paul boldly declared to them, "What therefore you worship as unknown, this I proclaim to you" (Acts 17:23). In other words, "What you think is unknowable, I am here to tell you is *knowable*." From the beginning of human history, God has revealed himself to us in nature (via providence), and now in these last days, he has revealed himself to us in Christ Jesus.

Moreover, by declaring who this ultimate being is, Paul identified God in nine ways that undermined the Greeks' philosophical conception of God (Acts 17:23–31). From natural revelation, Paul claimed that

1. God is knowable (v. 23),
2. God is the creator of the universe (v. 24a),
3. God is ontologically distinct from the universe (v. 24b),
4. God is self-contained (v. 25),
5. God is the governor of the universe (v. 26),
6. God is personal (v. 27a),
7. God is immanent (v. 27b), and
8. God is the judge (v. 31a).

And from special revelation, Paul claimed that God is the God of the miraculous (v. 31b).

In the process of declaring who this God is, Paul cited one of their poets, Aratus. It appears that Paul did this to demonstrate the inherent inconsistency and the internal absurdity of their own pagan worldview. Aratus believed, as with all those present at Mars Hill, that mankind was the offspring of the unknowable God because mankind, as with all other things, ontologically flows from the being of the unknowable God. Aratus supposed that we are connected to the unknown God through the gods. And the king of the gods, who ruled Mount Olympus, was Zeus. Because all things flow from the unknowable

God through the gods, all things remain a part of God. Deity exists in everyone and in everything. This is seen in the poem Paul cited:

> Let us begin with Zeus,
> whom we mortals never leave unspoken.
> For every street, every market-place
> is full of god.
> Even the sea and the harbour
> are full of this deity.
> Everywhere everyone is indebted to god.
> For we are indeed his offspring.

By citing the line, "For we are indeed his offspring," Paul showed the utter folly of idol worship: "Being then God's offspring, we ought not to think that the divine being is like gold or silver or stone, an image formed by the art and imagination of man" (v. 29). Clearly, graven images are the by-product of the creativity and "imagination" of men. And it does not make sense for men to worship something they created. Because it is "in him we live and move and have our being" (v. 28), it is not rational for us to worship graven images that depend on us for their existence rather than worshiping God, on whom we depend for our existence.

But in all this, Paul contrasted their impersonal, deistic, and unknowable god (who completely stays unconcerned and unaware and apathetic toward the universe) with the personal and immanent and knowable God of natural and special revelation (who is very much concerned with all the affairs of men). The God who has revealed himself, Paul says, is the God of divine providence. He is not the God who is far off but the God who is near and cares (v. 27a). He is the personal creator, provider, and judge who seeks to be sought after and found (v. 27b).

And if these truths (from natural revelation) alone didn't totally deconstruct their philosophical worldview, he added one more truth (from special revelation) to finish it off. Not only is God knowable, personal, and immanent, he is supernaturally present in the miraculous resurrection of Jesus Christ from the dead (v. 31). Because there is obviously no place for any supernatural interaction in a materialistic worldview, this led many of Paul's hearers to mock and ridicule him (v. 32).

Nevertheless, Paul didn't redeem Epicureanism or Stoicism or polytheism or Greek philosophy. Rather, Paul deconstructed the foundation of their worldview entirely. And at the same time, while reducing their worldview to absurdity, Paul appealed to natural revelation to bring his hearers to a proper knowledge of God so he could conclude with the special revelation—the gospel—that Christ was supernaturally resurrected from the dead.

In sum, the apostle Paul was not an advocate of Greek philosophy. Not at all. If Aristotle is so important, why didn't Paul point Christians to his writings? Instead, Paul did the opposite. He told Christians to beware of the philosophies and traditions of men (Col 2:8). In fact, he claimed that philosophy was not needed to know God, for God has clearly revealed himself to all mankind (Romans 1). Moreover, it was the wisdom of God, Paul said, that makes it impossible for men—if they do not, in fear, submit to what they already know to be true—to come to a proper knowledge of God in their own (so-called) wisdom (1 Cor 1:21).

6

THEOLOGIANS WHO REJECTED AQUINAS'S NATURAL THEOLOGY

Even if there is some truth relayed in Greek philosophy, Greek philosophy, as a whole, is only as good as its starting presuppositions. And because Greek philosophy relies on the wisdom of man rather than the wisdom of God (divine revelation), it is, in all its various forms, fatally flawed. When we look to the wisdom of men to know God, our doctrine of God will become distorted and vexed with all types of irresolvable contradictions. If we don't build our knowledge of God on divine revelation alone, we shouldn't expect to come to the same God of revelation. I agree with Tertullian: "What indeed does Athens have to do with Jerusalem? What concord is there between the Academy and the Church?"[1]

Theophilus of Antioch

Yet before Tertullian made his famous remarks against pagan philosophy, Theophilus of Antioch made his own disparaging statements against the wisdom flowing out of Athens:

> To be sure, many writers have imitated it and have desired to compose a narrative about these matters [the Scriptural account of creation], but, although they derived their starting-point from it in dealing with the creation of the world or the nature of man, what they said did not contain even a slight spark worthy of truth. What has been said by philosophers, historians, and poets is thought to be trustworthy because of its embellished style, but what they say is proved foolish and pointless by abundance of their nonsense and the absence of even the slightest measure of the truth in their writings. Even if something true seems to have been proclaimed by them, it is mixed with error. Just as some deadly poison when mixed with honey or wine anything else makes the whole harmful and useless; so their lo-

---

[1] Tertullian, *De praescriptione haereticorum* (*The Prescription Against Heretics*), chap. 8.

quacity is found to be pointless labour and causes harm to those who are persuaded by it.[2]

Martin Luther

Martin Luther, a student of Aristotle, agreed with Theophilus and Tertullian when he criticized the medieval Scholastics. In 1517, Harold Grimm claimed, "Luther was working on a commentary on the first book of Aristotle's Physics for the purpose of dethroning the god of the scholastics."[3] In another work published in September of that same year, *Disputation Against Scholastic Theology*, Luther wrote, "It is an error to say that no man can become a theologian without Aristotle." He went on to say, "Indeed, no one can become a theologian unless he becomes one without Aristotle."[4] Luther blamed the Scholastics for mixing "the dreams of Aristotle with theological matters, and conduct non-sensical disputations about the majesty of God, beyond and against the privilege granted them."[5] Concerning Aquinas in particu-

---

2 Robert M. Grant, *Theophilus of Antioch: Ad Autolycum: Text and Translation*, Oxford Early Christian Texts (Oxford: Oxford University Press, 1971), 2.12.

3 Harold J. Grimm, "Introduction to the 'Disputation Against Scholastic Theology,'" in *The Works of Martin Luther*, ed. Helmut T. Lehmann (Philadelphia: Fortress, 1957), 31:6.

4 Luther, *Disputation Against Scholastic Theology*, 42-43.

5 Martin Luther, 'Disputation on Indulgence, 1517," in *Works of Martin Luther* (Grand Rapids: Baker, 1915), 1.46.

lar, Luther claimed he was "the source and foundation of all heresy, error and obliteration of the Gospel."[6]

Philip Melanchthon

Luther's companion, Philip Melanchthon, was also critical of the Scholasticism of Thomas Aquinas.[7] "No faithful man," Melanchthon said, "has ever satisfied his mind with Scholastic theology, which has become polluted by so many human arguments, nonsense, tricks."[8] Melanchthon, recognizing that none of the Schoolmen based their theology on Scripture alone, said, "In the citadels of scholasticism, one learns theology not according to the Bible but according to the pronouncements of men."[9]

Huldreich Zwingli

Huldreich Zwingli had this to say about Greek philosophy:

> All, therefore, is sham and false religion

---

6 *Luther on Thomas Aquinas: The Angelic Doctor in the Thought of the Reformer*, trans. Denis Janz (Franz Steiner, 1989), 11.

7 See Philip Melanchthon, "Paul and the Scholastics," in *Melanchthon: Selected Writings*, 31–56.

8 Quoted in Charles Leander Hil, *Melanchthon: Selected Writing*, ed. E. E. Flack and L. M. Sa!re (Minneapolis: Augsburg Publishing House, 1962), 17–18.

9 Clyde Leonard Manschreck, *Melanchthon, The Quiet Reformer* (New York: Abingdon, 1958), 52.

that the theologians have adduced from philosophy as to what God is. If certain men have uttered certain truths on this subject, it has been from the mouth of God, who has scattered even among the heathen some seeds of the knowledge of Himself, though sparingly and darkly; otherwise they would not be true. But we, to whom God Himself has spoken through His Son and through the Holy Spirit, are to seek these things not from those who were puffed up with human wisdom, and consequently corrupted what they received pure, but from the divine oracles. For when men began to disregard these, they fell into all that is fleshly, i.e., into the inventions of philosophy, took to believing these, and, relying upon them, not only held such views as they liked about God, but forced others to hold the same. And this, though none of them would have permitted any one to hold such view of himself as that other, whoever he was, wished. Such is the arrogance of the flesh that gave itself out as theology. We wish to learn out of His own mouth what God is, lest we become corrupt and do abominable works. Psalm 14.[10]

Henry Bullinger

Like his friend Zwingli, Henry Bullinger criticized the Schoolmen for the same reason. Ac-

---

10 Huldreich Zwingli, *Commentary on True and False Religion in The Latin Works of Huldreich Zwingli*, ed. Clarence Nevin Heller (Philadelphia: Heidelberg, 1929), 3:62.

cording to Bullinger, the problem is that the Schoolmen did not limit their understanding of God to divine revelation. Bullinger levied this criticism while having a thorough knowledge of Aquinas's teaching. Before he embraced the doctrines of the Reformation, Bullinger studied at the oldest college in Cologne, Bursa Montis. At this renowned institution, Aristotle and Aquinas were the chief authorities. Yet Bullinger claimed, "Let this stand as it were for a continual rule, that God cannot be rightly known but by his word; and that God is to be received and believed to be such an one as he revealeth himself unto us in this holy word. For no creature verily can better tell what, and what kind of one God is, than God himself."[11]

John Calvin

John Calvin was also no friend of Aquinas, according to the historian of the Swiss Reformation, Bruce Gordon.[12] William Bouwsma asserts that Calvin's "sharpest attacks on philosophy were directed against Scholasticism as the most flagrant example of the attempt of philosophers to storm heaven."[13] In response to the extrabiblical

---

11 Henry Bullinger, *The Decades of Henry Bullinger*, 4.3 (2:125).

12 See Bruce Gordon, *Calvin* (New Haven, CT: Yale University Press, 2009), 62.

13 Bouwsma, *John Calvin*, 156.

philosophizing of the Schoolmen, Calvin countered that "God 'does not wish us to be too wise' but to exhibit 'sobriety': we must not seek to know more than 'it pleases him to teach us.' When he 'is our teacher and we hear him speak, he is able to give us prudence and discretion to understand his teaching, and we cannot fail in that; but when our Lord keeps his mouth closed, we must also keep our senses closed and hold them captive.'"[14]

John Owen

John Owen was also no fan of integrating Greek philosophy with theology, claiming that "biblical truth itself has absolutely nothing in common with secular philosophy."[15] He continues,

> We must consider philosophy as it has been developed and polished by generations of thinkers who were ignorant of God and His will. This is quite another matter and its encroachment into theology must be called into question. Shall philosophy be suffered to mingle its principles, notions, hypotheses, and conclusions with the teaching of the gospel and bring into it methods, means, and conclusions which are subservient to the naked human intellect? Shall philosophers be allowed to employ their reasoning and methodolo-

---

14 Bouwsma, 156.

15 John Owen, *Biblical Theology* (Morgan, PA: Soli Deo Gloria, 2002), 670.

gy to the interpretation, declaration, and teaching of Christian doctrine as they have reined them according to their own discretion and schools of thought?[16]

Owen blamed Aquinas and the Schoolmen for polluting theology with pagan philosophy:

> Once philosophy had gained a foothold in the schools of Christ, then the knowledge of God in Christ Jesus quietly withdrew as was predicted by the Spirit in the Scriptures, and confirmed in the experience of many. The most special and virulent poison to bring about this effect was the Aristotelian or Peripatetic philosophy which, having lain neglected for some centuries, began again to please men devoted to "literary pursuits." In fact, it had been preserved and cultivated by the Mohammedan Arabs, and now it invaded the Christian world as quickly as it could be transmitted by word of mouth. That philosophy, especially as refined and transmitted by Arabs, was a most apt and subtle medium for generating divisions and for instigating lawsuits, controversies, and quarrels about anything at all your please. Adopting and relying on this, the scholastics, in effect, replaced the norm and faith of evangelical theology with a barbarous and philosophical pseudo-scientific "learning." Who will deny that the subject matter of scholastic theology . . . is but the

---

16 Owen, 669.

boilings-down of Aristotelian metaphysics applied to the discussion of supernatural affairs? . . . Wherever they hold up their perverse and improper speculations and interpretations, it is always the name of Aristotle that they shelter behind.[17]

Francis Turretin

Though Francis Turretin claimed philosophy had a place as an aid to theology (as the Bible itself answers all the major philosophical questions to provide us a holistic worldview), he made it clear that Greek philosophy "contains many errors and . . . is of no use but of the greatest harm. Thus Paul condemns it (Col. 2:8)."[18]

With this in mind, Turretin blamed the Schoolmen, along with some of the Church Fathers, for falsely introducing the errors of Aristotelian philosophy into theology: "Some of the fathers, coming out from among the philosophers, still retained some frothier erroneous opinions and endeavored to bring the Gentiles over to Christianity by a mixture of philosophical and theological doctrines: as Justin Martyr, Origen, Clement of Alexandria, and the Scholastics, whose system is of Aristotle or other philosophers

---

17 Owen, 676.

18 Francis Turretin, *Institutes of Elenctic Theology*, ed. James Dennison Jr., trans. George Musgrave Giger (Phillipsburg, NJ: P&R, 1992), 1:44–45.

than upon the testimonies of the prophets and apostles."[19]

John Gill

Likewise, John Gill did not mince words when he attacked the Schoolmen: "The race of schoolmen a few centuries ago, who introduced the philosophy of Aristotle, Averroes, and others, into all the subjects of divinity: to observe no more, such kind of philosophy is here meant, which may be truly called vain deceit: that is, that which is vain and empty, and has no solid foundation, even in nature and reason itself; and which being applied to divine things and religious observances, is deceitful and delusory: after the tradition of men."[20]

Objections

David Haines claims that the Reformers and those who followed them were essentially in agreement with Aquinas: "Aquinas says about natural theology and compares it with the writings of most of the Reformed theologians from the 1500s to the end of the 1800s, we will find that they are in substantial agreement."[21] Yet Haines fails to realize

---

19 Turretin, 1:44.

20 John Gill, *Commentary on Colossians 2:8*, Bible Study Tools, accessed December 2, 2021, https://www.biblestudytools.com/commentaries/gills-exposition-of-the-bible/colossians-2-8.html.

21 Haines, *Natural Theology*, 9.

the key difference between holding to a natural theology tied to natural revelation and the natural theology of Aquinas, which is tied to Greek philosophy. And it is certain that the Reformers rejected the natural theology of Aquinas and the Greek philosophy in which it was rooted.

What about all the sixteenth- and seventeenth-century Protestant scholars who appealed to Aristotle via Aquinas? Undoubtedly, some post-Reformation Protestants, such as Peter Martyr Vermigli, drew from Aquinas to integrate Aristotelian philosophy into their theology. But, as John Owen emphasized, this is not because they were following the Reformers. Though the Reformers rightfully rejected Aquinas and Aristotle, regrettably, not all those who came after them followed their example:

> In the last century, it pleased God to bring in a reformation of the churches in several European nations, and they in turn began to radiate the light and truth of Christ by preaching the gospel in its power and simplicity. At the same time, it became an abomination and an object of hatred to many good and pious men to see the hold that the schools and academies of philosophy had over the minds of men. But now, with the passing of the years, whether the learned men and the teachers of the Reformed Churches have remained

> free from the contagion is something that each must decide for himself.
>
> I shall merely cite what Johann Drusius says in his comment on those words of Peter that "the dog is turned to his vomit again" (2 Peter 2:22). Says he, "Such are those who now turn to the things that the first Reformers vomited out, which things include the scholastic theology."[22]

In the end, Owen blamed Thomas and the Schoolmen for infecting theology with the poison of philosophy: "From the date when the disputes, nay, the obscurities of the scholastics began to come to the fore, sacred theology became more and more besmirched and contaminated with worldly philosophy."[23]

Conclusion

Distinctions matter in historical theology. Just because Reformation and post-Reformation Protestant theologians held to natural revelation does not mean they were in agreement with the philosophical theology of Thomas Aquinas.

---

22 Owen, *Biblical Theology*, 677–678.
23 Owen, 677.

Conclusion

Because of the influence of Aquinas, I am not convinced that natural theology is worth saving. Like Joel Beeke and Paul Smalley, I would personally prefer to uphold natural revelation over against natural theology.[1] When it comes to the knowledge of God, I am not sure what more can be included in natural theology than that which is clearly revealed in natural revelation.

But if we are going to save the term *natural theology*, we must make sure that what we are saving is rooted in natural revelation and not natural science. And we must be careful not to allow the influence of pagan philosophy to enter our natural

---

[1] Beeke and Smalley: "We must not attempt a natural theology that sets up human reason as the authority" (*Reformed Systematic Theology*, 1:241). Consequently, Beeke and Smalley "believe that the best approach to these matters is to affirm general revelation and yet avoid natural theology" (1:236).

theology. Pagan philosophy, in all of its various forms, is a rejection and suppression of natural theology. It replaces the self-contained God of providence with an abstract being that cannot be ontologically distinguished from the universe.

Thus, we must be careful not to base any aspect of our doctrine of God on something not taught in Scripture, such as the pantheistic concept of divine immobility. We must keep in mind that whatever is revealed in nature about God is also revealed in the Bible. It's dangerous to believe anything about God, such as divine immobility, not taught in Holy Scripture. It is for this reason that pagan philosophy is no handmaiden to theology. The Bible is sufficient in revealing all we need to know about God.

In short, the natural theology of Thomas Aquinas was not constructed on natural revelation. Instead, he built his natural theology on the physics and metaphysics of Aristotle. The failure of the natural theology of Thomas Aquinas is not that he sought to construct a theology outside of special revelation but that he sought to build a theology outside of natural revelation. Rather than starting on the knowledge of God, which is freely and universally revealed to us (the true foundation of all knowledge), Thomas pushed that method of knowing God aside and sought to construct his own way to God on the foundation of Greek philosophy. His failure was that he looked to pagan philosophy rather than to God's revelation. Thus, in seeking to save natural theology from Aquinas, I am seeking to save natural theology from the deistic and pantheistic god of Greek philosophy.

The case I am making is not an attack on reason, for I seek to use reason against the reasoning of Aquinas. Neither am I attacking science or metaphysics. I am not even denying the importance of answering philosophical questions, as the Bible offers us a philosophical worldview that answers all our ontological, epistemological, and ethical questions (for more on that, see my book *The Absurdity of Unbelief*[2]).

The thrust of this book, as well as that of *The Failure of Natural Theology*, is an attack on the notion that man can intellectually work his way to the knowledge of God without first submitting to that knowledge constantly communicated to him within the "theater of God's glory."

Sadly, as it was in the days of John Owen, a trend is ensuing to push the philosophical theology of the quintessential Catholic theologian on the evangelical Protestant church. And with Owen, I find this trend to be extremely dangerous.

---

2 Conway, AR: Free Grace Press, 2016.

Baptizing Aristotle through the Dominican hands of Aquinas does not sanctify the pagan philosopher; it only paganizes our knowledge of God. To keep our knowledge of God pure, may we restrict our understanding of him to what has been disclosed in natural revelation and confirmed and expanded within Holy Scripture.

If this makes me a biblicist, then I am guilty as charged.

On Campus & Distance Options Available

GRACE BIBLE
THEOLOGICAL SEMINARY

Interested in becoming a student
or supporting our ministry?
Please visit gbtseminary.org

www.ingramcontent.com/pod-product-compliance
Lightning Source LLC
Chambersburg PA
CBHW031455040426
42444CB00007B/1103